To

....

....

From

....

....

....

To Elliott and Austin with love

Text copyright © 2022 Kenneth Steven
Illustrations by Katie Rewse
This edition copyright © 2022 Lion Hudson IP Limited

The right of Kenneth Steven to be identified as the author of this work has been asserted by him in accordance with the Copyright, Designs and Patents Act 1988.

All rights reserved. No part of this publication may be reproduced or transmitted in any form or by any means, electronic or mechanical, including photocopy, recording, or any information storage and retrieval system, without permission in writing from the publisher.

Published by **Lion Children's Books**
www.lionhudson.com
Part of the SPCK Group
SPCK, 36 Causton Street, London, SW1P 4ST

ISBN 978 0 7459 7897 0

First edition 2022

Acknowledgments

Scripture quotations are taken from the Holy Bible, New International Version Anglicised. Copyright © 1979, 1984, 2011 Biblica, formerly International Bible Society. Used by permission of Hodder & Stoughton Ltd, an Hachette UK company. All rights reserved. "NIV" is a registered trademark of Biblica. UK trademark number 1448790.

A catalogue record for this book is available from the British Library

Printed and bound in China, April 2022, LH54

Blessings
FOR YOUR
BAPTISM

By Kenneth Steven
Illustrated by Katie Rewse

There is so much we want to give you,
but most of all we want to give you this blessing.
It comes with all the love in our hearts.

May you be blessed by the early morning light that flows through the valley and wakens the meadow and trees,

May you be blessed by the river as it journeys from the hills to the sea,

babbling its stories as it splashes your growing feet.

May you be blessed by the soft rain as it falls in a song on the grass and the leaves and the roofs,

May you be blessed by the sea as the waves
curl blue and green far out,

May you be blessed by the rainbow that arches over the fields in promise after the rain has cleared,

showing that the sun will always come back, so you can go out to play once more.

May you be blessed by the snow that drifts like petals on the wind, and settles in every crack and crevice,

and makes the world white,
for you to slide and skate and sledge.

May you be blessed by the stars
that sparkle in the night skies
in their millions,
shining like silver breath
from north to south,
and east to west.

May you be blessed by God, who made all these things for us to look after,

and to love and delight in all the days of our lives.

Our words of blessing to you:

Let the heavens rejoice, let the earth be glad;
   let the sea resound, and all that is in it.
Let the fields be jubilant, and everything in them;
   let all the trees of the forest sing for joy.

Psalm 96:11-12

You will go out in joy
    and be led forth in peace;
the mountains and hills
    will burst into song before you,
and all the trees of the field
    will clap their hands.

Isaiah 55:12

The Lord bless you
   and keep you;
the Lord make his face shine on you
   and be gracious to you;
the Lord turn his face towards you
   and give you peace.

Numbers 6:24-26